DATE DUE			

NOV 03 '89

A True Adventure
THE STORY OF THREE WHALES

Weather
Today: Partly sunny and cooler.
High 62. Low 44. Wind 7-14 mph.
Thursday: Mostly sunny and cool.
High 60. Wind 6-12 mph.
Yesterday: AQI: 35. Temp. range;
58-70. Details on Page D2.

The Washington Post

FINAL

Detailed index on Page A2

111TH YEAR · · · · No. 319 · · · © 1988, The Washington Post Company   WEDNESDAY, OCTOBER 19, 1988   K   Prices May Vary in Areas Outside Metropolitan Washington (See Box on A4)   25¢

Whale Rescuers Race the Clock

Icebreaker's Trip Delayed

By Bruce Bartley
Associated Press

BARROW, Alaska, Oct. 18—Freezing temperatures, erratic winds and shifting ice shut off all escape routes today for three stranded California gray whales as rescuers prepared for a dangerous attempt to free them.

The rescue effort, which hangs on the arrival of an icebreaking barge from Prudhoe Bay, has become a race against time. The young whales are exhausted from fighting the current to stay beneath gaps in the ice where they could surface for air. At least one of the whales may have pneumonia. Their barnacled snouts are raw from grating on the jagged ice.

At Prudhoe Bay, about 200 miles southeast, an Army National Guard Skycrane helicopter was ready to hook a 185-ton icebreaking hovercraft barge owned by VECO Inc. and tow it across the Arctic Ocean to the whales at Point Barrow.

But late tonight, the trip was put on hold until Wednesday morning. The journey was delayed when the barge became stuck in the ice, then for refueling before the barge was moved a short distance.

Col. Tom Carroll of the Alaska Army National Guard said the barge was pulled from the dock but it moved slowly.

Mike Haller, a National Guard spokesman,
See WHALES, A16, Col. 1

Biologist Geoff Carroll, in white parka, stands with Eskimos near breathing hole used by trapped whales. Nearest open sea is 200 miles away.

Hill Creates Department For Veterans

Senate Also Approves More Disability Aid, GI Appellate Court

By Tom Kenworthy
Washington Post Staff Writer

The Senate last night handed the nation's 27 million veterans a triple victory, enacting legislation to create a Cabinet department for veterans affairs and passing other measures to raise disability benefits and set up a new federal court where veterans can appeal denials of benefits.

All three measures were approved by voice votes as the Senate mopped up last-minute legislative details prior to the 100th Congress' expected adjournment later this week or early next week. The Senate continued intermittent negotiations on the two major pieces of legislative business remaining: an omnibus antidrug act and a bill making technical corrections to the 1986 Tax Reform Act.

The compromise measure elevating the Veterans Administration to Cabinet level effective next March was approved by the House two weeks ago and now goes to Pres-

The Washington Post

FINAL

Detailed index on Page A2

Weather

Today: Mostly sunny and mild. High 60, Low 44. Wind 6-12 mph.
Friday: Mostly cloudy with scattered showers. High 62.
...day: AQI: 30 Temp. range: ...lls on Page C2.

THURSDAY, OCTOBER 27, 1988

No. 327   © 1988, The Washington Post Company   25¢

Prices May Vary in Areas Outside Metropolitan Washington (See Box on A2)

...les Head for Sea—With Help From Friends

Repelled attempts to break through ice have left animals battered and weak.

Whales must surface to breathe, but holes in the ice are shrinking.

GRAY WHALES

Description: Medium-sized whales. Can grow to be 45-feet long and weigh up to 40.8 tons. Gestation lasts 11-12 months.

Habitat: Found off the coast of southern California and Baja California between November and May. Most move north in springtime to the Bering Sea where the herd divides, half travels toward the Siberian coast and half moves north into the Arctic Ocean. Return trip begins toward the end of September. Whales lingering in the Arctic risk being trapped by ice.

Feeding: Gray whales travel to Arctic waters to feed, mainly on small crabs.

Population: Completely protected since 1937 when hunting helped reduce the worldwide population to about 250. Current population is about 21,000.

SOURCE: Grolier's Animal Life Encyclopedia

Three whales are trapped, one adult, one young adult and one 2-year-old.

Rescuers, who called off their surveillance of the whales at dark tonight, last saw the two at 7 p.m. surfacing in holes in open water with icy rubble around them. The Soviet icebreakers, flying both the Stars and Stripes and the hammer and sickle, were continuing to work tonight to keep the channel clear. Rescuers said they would be unable to tell before dawn Thursday whether the whales plunged through the last of the ice chunks

... Oct. 26—
... the manpower of
... two Soviet
... Eskimos opened
... miles of ice today
... trapped whales and

... ree weeks after they
... overed icebound off
... rrow, the two whales
... atted about 4 p.m. local
... running in a newly formed
... toward the demolished
... ns of a 35-foot-high ice ridge
... had been the last obstacle to
... ir release, Lt. Mike Haller of
... Alaska Army National Guard
... aid.

"We'll monitor them from whichever way we can to ensure that they don't turn around and come back to thank us," National Guard Sgt. Ian Robertson joked. But the whales, whom biologists had named Crossbeak and Bonnet, were not tagged and would be on their own for the long swim to their breeding grounds in California.

An Eskimo pets whale before it joined companion in swimming along path created for them in Arctic ice before it headed for open seas.

into the lead system through which they could swim to open ocean.

All day long, the animals seemed to sense that their ordeal was almost over.

One behind the other, the two freedom-bound gray whales threaded a path toward the ridge from breathing hole to breathing hole cut for them in the ice by man and machine. Onlookers dashed ahead, watching the openings for the tell-tale swell of water that signaled the whales progress.

Every few moments, the whales lunged from the water, their tiny eyes barely visible above the surface before they slipped again under the ice. "The whales are up and active today," Lt. Mike Haller of the Alaska Army National Guard said. "They've got their luggage packed, and they're ready to go."

They weren't the only ones. As dawn crept across the ice Wednesday, scores of people flocked to the rescue site, hoping to witness

See WHALES, A4, Col. 1

Demolition Of Embassy Supported

President to Urge Replacing Bugged Structure in Moscow

By Don Oberdorfer
Washington Post Staff Writer

President Reagan has decided to recommend that the United States tear down the nearly complete U.S. Embassy office building in Moscow and build another one on the same site under heavy security in the most expensive diplomatic construction project in U.S. history, administration officials said yesterday.

Reagan's decision, which State Department sources said they expect will be announced today, is the first official step toward erecting a new U.S. structure that may cost as much as $300 million. At least $22 million has already been spent on the building that is to be razed because U.S. officials fear it is riddled with sophisticated eavesdropping devices.

Officials said last night that because a design for a new U.S. building in Moscow has not been started, there is no reliable estimate of how long it will take to raze the current building, which was mostly completed by 1985, and build the new one. However, a knowledgeable official said the job would probably take five years, which would be a full decade after the scheduled 1983 completion of a structure that

---

Rescuers Race the Clock As Three Whales Weaken

Arctic Ocean

Barrow

Chukchi Sea

SOVIET UNION

U.S.

Beaufort Sea

Prudhoe Bay

Whales trapped here.

U.S. / CANADA

Arctic Circle

Fairbanks

ALASKA

NORTHWEST TERRITORIES

YUKON

Anchorage

Gulf of Alaska

BRITISH COLUMBIA

Prohibited Islands

North Pacific Ocean

CANADA

UNITED STATES

ALASKA

MILES 300

BY WARD SUTTON—THE WASHINGTON POST

WHALES, From A1

said crews would work through the ... to lighten the barge by remov... ing fuel.

"We're looking at seeing if it ... makes things a little smoother," he ... said. "We'll go after it again at first ... light tomorrow."

The whales were hemmed in nearly two weeks ago while migrat...

swim south to California and Mex... ico before the winter weather roots the Arctic Ocean with a vast slab of ice.

Whale biologists said it is likely that, of the thousands of whales that summer in the Arctic, a few start the journey south too late and drown because the ice locks them off. This year, it happened only a few hundred feet offshore, near...

... produced Thursday.

... California is the ... ... ously to stay alive. ... supply. Because the ... are as low as 17 degrees below ... Fahrenheit, the holes are freezing ... shut.

Observers said the whales usu...

must swim upstream almost contin... uously to stay alive.

Although considered an endan... gered species, the California gray whale population, currently about 21,000, is believed to be increasing at about 2.5 percent per year, a

that they are tiring and must breathe harder to stay alive.

Although considered an endan... gered species, the California gray whale population, currently about 21,000, is believed to be increasing at about 2.5 percent per year, a

A True Adventure

THE STORY OF THREE WHALES

WRITTEN BY GILES WHITTELL ILLUSTRATED BY PATRICK BENSON

Gareth Stevens Children's Books
MILWAUKEE

Library of Congress Cataloging-in-Publication Data
Whittell, Giles.
The story of three whales.
Summary: Describes how the concerted efforts of an international team of concerned people eased the suffering of
three gray whales trapped by ice off the coast of Alaska and eventually helped two of them back to the open sea.
1. Pacific gray whale--Alaska--Juvenile literature.
2. Wildlife rescue--Alaska--Juvenile literature.
3. Mammals--Alaska--Juvenile literature. [1. Pacific
gray whale. 2. Whales. 3. Wildlife rescue] I. Benson, Patrick, ill. II. Title.
QL737.C425W47   1989   599.5'1   88-35630
ISBN 0-8368-0067-2   ISBN 0-8368 0092-3 (lib. bdg.)   ISBN 0-8368-0093-1 (softcover)

age 9-12

North American edition first published in 1989 by Gareth Stevens, Inc., 7317 West Green Tree Road, Milwaukee, WI 53223
First published 1988 by Telegraph Books/Walker Books. Text © 1988 Giles Whittell. Illustrations © 1988 Patrick Benson.

For twelve bright weeks every summer, the Arctic Ocean is full of life. Blooms of plankton float among the icebergs. Shellfish slide along the sea floor. Squid lurk under pitch-black overhangs of rock. And whales swim up from the Pacific to feed.

Humpback whales, Bowhead whales and California Gray whales all come to the Arctic. In the summer of 1988 one particular herd of California Grays was plunging and rolling, leaping and belly-flopping, off the north coast of Alaska.

But winter came early in 1988. The first sign was a freezing wind from the east. Blizzards blew in from the top of the world. Thick pack-ice spread out from the shore and its shadow fell over the whales.

Most of the whales were quick to sense the changes. In small groups, they set off on the long swim south to warmth for the winter. But three of the whales failed to notice the end of summer – one adult, one middle-sized, one baby.

Quietly the ice crept in. The ocean was changing from blue to silent white. Gray whales can hold their breath under water for half an hour, but soon the three who had been left behind would have nowhere left to surface.

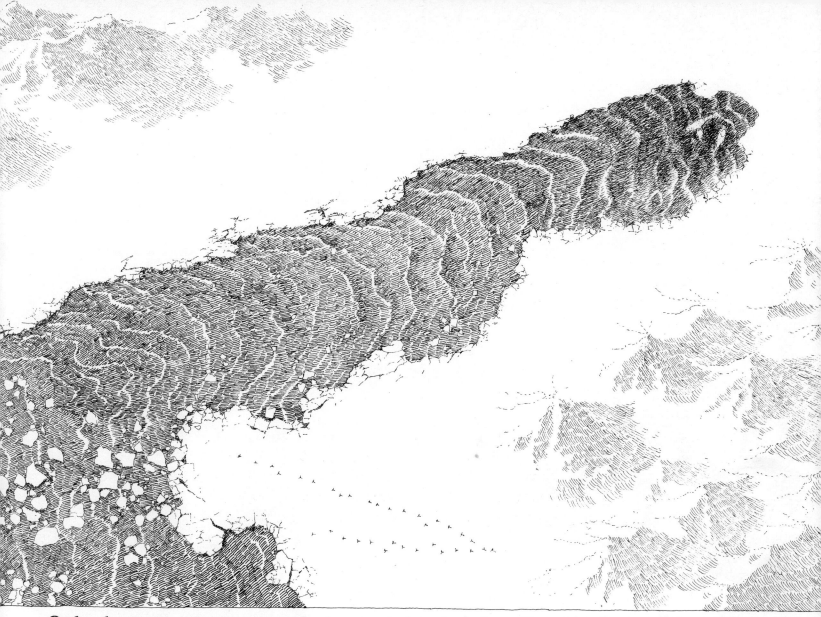

Only the open water was safe, beyond the pack-ice. But the three whales lost their sense of direction. They swam toward land, into an Alaskan bay, where the still, shallow water was certain to freeze very quickly.

At the mouth of the bay was a shelf of ice, under water. Broken pack-ice piled up against it, forming a wall. From sea-bed to surface there was no way out.

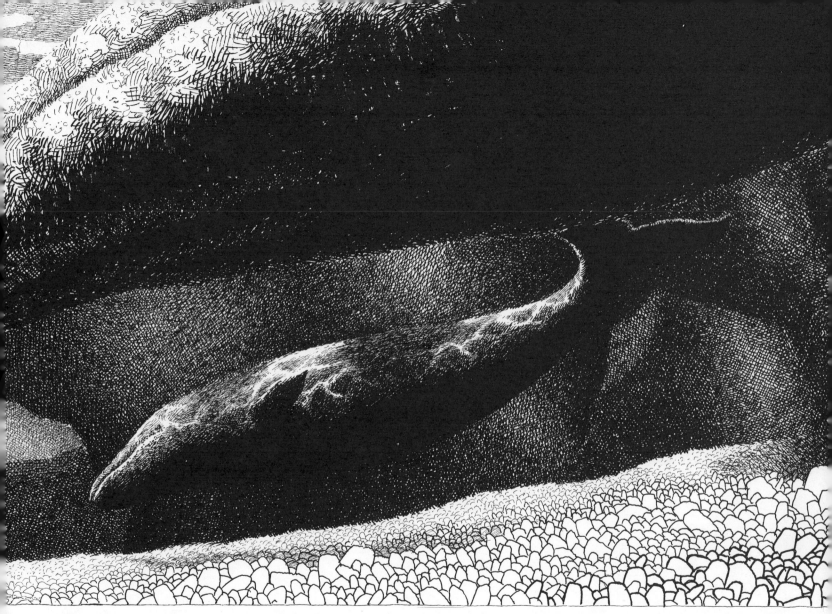

Then the surface froze solid. The whales were trapped in a prison of ice. They could not breathe. Again and again they rammed upward at the ice with their noses.

At last they managed to push their great heads through a crack in the ice. An Inuit hunter was passing and saw them. In nearby Barrow, an Inuit town, he told people what he had seen.

To begin with nothing was done to save the whales. It would be natural
for the whales to die and the Inuit accepted it. But the news of the whales
began to spread. Their pictures appeared on local TV.

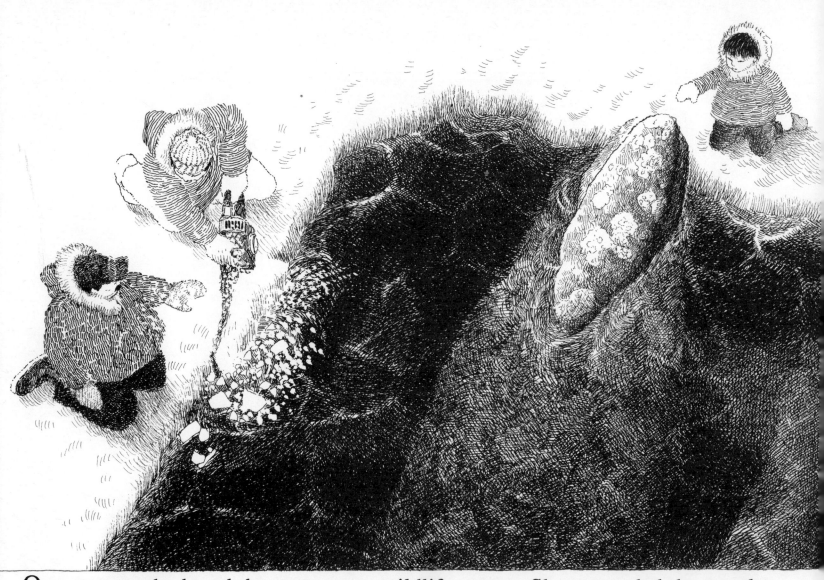

One person who heard the news was a wildlife ranger. She persuaded the people of Barrow to help keep the whales alive. Out over the ice they trudged, with axes, ice-poles and chainsaws to cut breathing holes.

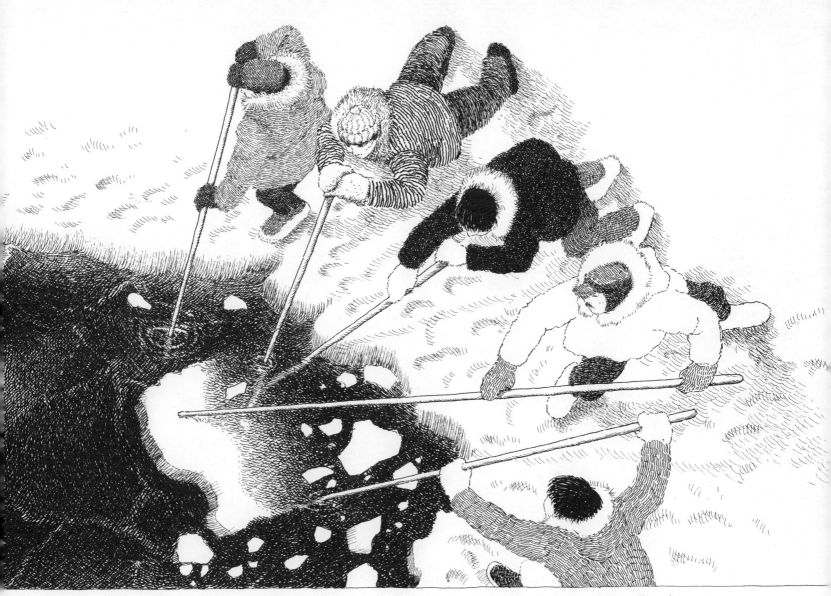

The whales appeared at the holes and filled their huge lungs. The Inuit gave them names: Siku (the biggest), Poutu (the middle one) and Kannick (the baby). *Siku* means ice in Inuit. *Poutu* means ice-hole and *Kannick* means snowflake.

The Inuit cut a line of breathing holes, out toward the open water. They worked for fourteen days and nights. Clattering chainsaws sliced constantly through the ice, but the water would quickly freeze solid again.

Siku, Poutu and Kannick refused to follow the line of holes. They stayed by the shore where they knew they could breathe. "The Plight of the Whales" became front-page news all over the world. Millions of people waited in hope.

From all across America, offers of help poured in. But nothing could break through the wall of ice at the mouth of the bay. An enormous bulldozer tried, but stuck fast.

A sky-crane helicopter hammered the ice with a concrete torpedo. It punched a line of holes from the whales to the wall. But still the whales wouldn't follow.

Their noses were bloody and scraped to the bone. The ice was invincible. It seemed to the watching world that the whales must die. Polar bears stalked the ice, waiting patiently for a feast of whale-meat.

One evening Siku and Poutu surfaced alone. Being the smallest, Kannick was also the weakest. Morning came and still only Siku and Poutu appeared at the hole. No one could say exactly what had happened. And no one ever saw Kannick again.

On the twentieth day, Siku and Poutu felt the tremble of distant engines. A huge Russian ice-breaker was roaring to the rescue, the great *Admiral Makarov*.

The captain found a grand phrase to mark the occasion. "Let us begin to break ice!" he called. All night the breaker charged at the ice, pulled back, and charged again.

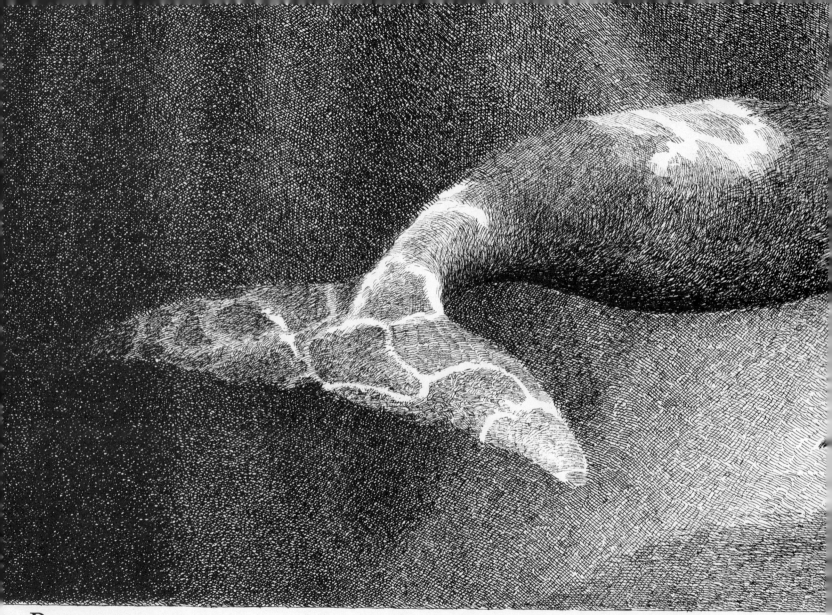

By morning a channel was clear, a quarter of a mile wide. The crew of the
Admiral Makarov grinned. They came ashore to celebrate and the Inuit
and other Americans hugged them and cheered.

Then the ice-breaker turned for the open sea with Siku and Poutu close behind.
The whales understood that they must follow the thunder and froth of the engines.
The sound would lead them from the prison of ice, to the open water and freedom.

The rest of the herd was three weeks ahead on the journey south. Siku and Poutu
had thousands of miles to swim. So they each blew a great waterspout and set off.
Their long ordeal was over now.

To Learn More About the World's Seas, About Whales, and Other Sea Animals . . .

Organizations

The two whales in this true story were saved because people cared and people cooperated — among them, local people in government, Americans, Canadians, and Soviets. Other people around the world want to protect nature. Some are especially interested in saving whales. Write to the addresses below to find out more. People there will send you information about saving whales and other wild species and about preserving nature.

Children of the Green Earth
P. O. Box 95219
Seattle, WA 98145

Greenpeace U.S.A.
1611 Connecticut Avenue NW
Washington, DC 20009

National Council for
   Environmental Balance
P. O. Box 7732
4169 Westport Road
Louisville, KY 40207

Save the Whales
P. O. Box 3650
Washington, DC 20007

Sierra Club
730 Polk Street
San Francisco, CA 94109

National Wildlife Federation
1412 16th Street NW
Washington, DC 20036

Wildlife Preservation Trust
   International
34th Street and Girard Avenue
Philadelphia, PA 19104

World Wildlife Fund
1250 24th Street NW, Suite 500
Washington, DC 20037

Books

The books listed below will tell you more about whales and other sea animals. Check your local library or bookstore to see if they have them or can order them for you.

Nonfiction —
Catch a Whale by the Tail. Ricciuti (Harper & Row)
A First Look at Whales. Selsam and Hunt (Walker & Co.)
Gentle Giants of the Sea. Whale Museum (Whale Museum)
Little Whale. McGovern (Scholastic)
Sharks and Whales. Albert (Putnam)

Whale and Dolphin. Serventy (Raintree)
Whales. Harris (Franklin Watts)
Whales and Dolphins. Sabin (Troll)
Whalewatch! Behrens (Childrens Press)

Fiction —
Amos and Boris. Steig (Farrar, Straus & Giroux)
Chasing Whales off Norway. Boschini and Boschini (Scroll)
Dale the Whale. Reese (Childrens Press)
Mabel the Whale. King (Modern Curriculum)
Manny's Whale. Starbuck (Dillon)

Rock-A-Bye Whale. Strange (Manzanita Press)
Stanley Bagshaw and the Twenty-Two Ton Whale.
   Wilson (David & Charles)
The Tale of Humphrey the Humpback Whale.
   Heus and Robinson (Brost-Heus)

A LIST OF WORDS ABOUT THE SEA

After each word from the story listed below, you can read what it means and see it used in a sentence.

bloom — a large growth of plankton that drift together on the water
A bloom of plankton drifted toward the shore.

concrete torpedo —a heavy stone device, like a wrecking ball, used to batter against something in order to make it crumble
The concrete torpedo was dropped again and again on the thick ice.

froth — a mass of bubbles found in or on top of a liquid
The froth from the boat's engines seemed warmer than the surrounding water.

herd — a number of creatures of the same kind that stay together in a group
A herd of animals often stays together in order to find food and raise the young in safety.

ice-breaker — a rugged ship built sturdy enough to break through ice on the seas
The ice-breaker slowly crawled through the Arctic night.

ice-pole — a sturdy pole with a pointed end made of metal used to chip into the ice
An Inuit uses both the ice-pole and the more modern tool, the chainsaw, when working on the ice.

Inuit— name of the Indian people living in northeastern Siberia, Greenland, and the Arctic region of North America. The Algonquian Indians, however, called the Inuit Eskimos, from their word *eskimantsik,* meaning "eaters of raw flesh."
The word Inuit means "the people."

pack-ice — floating ice that drifts together and moves as a large mass
In Labrador, children watch the seals playing on the pack-ice offshore.

plankton — plants and animals so tiny they can be seen in detail only with a microscope
Plankton float together in salt water or fresh water.

sky-crane — a device that works like a crane, moving and hoisting heavy objects on cables
A sky-crane is mounted on a helicopter so that it can be used in places that are otherwise hard for land equipment to reach.

squid — a sea creature with a long body, ten arms around its mouth, and a pair of fins on its tail
The squid, related to the octopus and cuttlefish, can reach 50 feet (15 m) in length and weigh 2 tons (1,814 kg).

waterspout —a jet of water that erupts from the blowhole, the top nostril, of a whale, when it surfaces for air
All that could be seen of the whale was its waterspout off in the distance.